JUL - 1 2016

3 1994 01551 4547

SANT

T1-AYB-735

D0116482

INNOVATION THROUGH ADVERSITY

DID ANYTHING GOOD COME OUT OF

THE COLD WAR?

PAUL MASON

ROSEN PUBLISHING

New York

J 909.825 MAS
Mason, Paul
Did anything good come out
of the Cold War?

$30.25
CENTRAL   31994015514547

Published in 2016 by The Rosen Publishing Group, Inc.
29 East 21st Street, New York, NY 10010

Copyright © 2016 Wayland/The Rosen Publishing Group, Inc

First Edition

All rights reserved. No part of this book may be reproduced in any form without permission in writing from the publisher, except by a reviewer.

Library of Congress Cataloging-in-Publication Data

Mason, Paul, 1967–
Did anything good come out of the Cold War? / Paul Mason.
pages cm.—(Innovation through adversity)
Includes bibliographical references and index.
ISBN 978-1-5081-7066-2 (library bound)
1. Cold War—Juvenile literature. 2. World politics—1945–1989—
Juvenile literature. I. Title.
D843.M257 2015
909.82'5—dc23
                                    2015023358

Manufactured in the United States of America

The publisher would like to thank the following for their kind permission to reproduce their photographs:

Key: (t) top; (c) center; (b) bottom; (l) left; (r) right

The following images are public domain: 5br, 7tr, 8br, 10bl, 10–11c, 15tl br, 16–17bc, 18bl tr, 19cl br, 21tr, 23tl bl, 26cl r, 32tr, 34cl, 36tl bl, 37 tr bl.

All other images istock.com unless otherwise indicated.

Front Cover bl, br Shutterstock.com, Back Cover cr NASA
4l br NASA, 4bl Shutterstock.com, 7c German Federal Archive, 13br Raphaël Thiémard, 14tl Vladimir Fedorenko, 21br Brian Minkoff-London Pixels. 29tr NASA, 30cr bl NASA, 30tl Wikimedia, 30cl Shutterstock.com, 31 tl cl bl br Shutterstock.com, 31bl cb NASA, 31cr Bettmann/Corbis, 33b Patrick Stollarz, 35t SRI International, 37tc SOVFOTO, 38bl Jeffchat1, 40bl Wolfgang Thieme, German Federal Archive, 41cl Getty Images, 41cr Dutch National Archive, 41br Gary Abraham, 42 Jiri Jiroutek, 43tl Israel Defense Forces, 44–45c Getty Images/Hulton Archive.
Every attempt has been made to clear copyright. Should there be any inadvertent omission, please apply to the publisher for rectification.

The website addresses (URLs) included in this book were valid at the time of going to press. However, it is possible that contents or addresses may have changed since the publication of this book. No responsibility for any such changes can be accepted by either the author or the Publisher.

METRIC CONVERSION CHARTS

1 inch = 2.54 centimeters	1 mile = 1.609 kilometers
1 foot = 30.48 centimeters	1 cup = 250 milliliters
1 yard = .914 meters	1 ounce = 28 grams
1 square foot = .093 square meters	1 fluid ounce = 30 milliliters
1 square mile = 2.59 square kilometers	1 teaspoon = 5 milliliters
1 ton = .907 metric tons	1 tablespoon = 15 milliliters
1 pound = 454 grams	355 degrees F = 180 degrees Celsius

CONTENTS

ACE TO THE MOON

In 1961, no one had ever been to the Moon. Few people even thought it was possible. But then US President John F. Kennedy made a famous speech. He said that the USA was going to send an astronaut to the Moon by 1970. The USA would start work right away, building rockets and space capsules.

Having become President in 1961, Kennedy served less than three years before he was assassinated in Dallas, Texas, in November 1963.

"WE CHOOSE TO GO TO THE MOON IN THIS DECADE AND DO THE OTHER THINGS, NOT BECAUSE THEY ARE EASY, BUT BECAUSE THEY ARE HARD."

President John F. Kennedy of the USA speaking in 1961, explaining the USA's determination to go to the Moon. Kennedy was suggesting that the difficult challenge of reaching the Moon would bring great rewards.

1957
USSR launches Sputnik, the first satellite to go into orbit around Earth.

1958
The National Aeronautics and Space Administration (NASA) is formed by the US government.

WHY VISIT THE MOON?

Just a few weeks before Kennedy's speech, cosmonaut Yuri Gagarin from the USSR had blasted into space and returned home alive. Gagarin was the first human ever to visit space.

The USA was shocked to find out that it was behind in what became known as the 'Space Race'. Kennedy was determined that the USA should catch up.

Both the USSR and USA developed powerful rockets to carry spacecraft and humans into orbit around Earth and beyond.

WHY DID THE SPACE RACE MATTER?

The Space Race mattered mostly because of the rivalry between the USA and the USSR. This rivalry was known as the Cold War.

The USA and the USSR each wanted other countries to be on its side, to gather bigger and more powerful forces to counter their opponents. The Space Race was a way of showing everyone who was best. To win, you needed better science, technology, industry, computers and astronaut-training than the other side. Having these might help to persuade other countries to join you.

The Space Race was only a small part of the Cold War, but it was an important one, because no one could argue with the results. The USSR had won the first stage, by putting the first human into space. President Kennedy had decided that the next step was the race to the Moon – and the USA was determined to win it.

1961
Yuri Gagarin of the USSR becomes the first human to go into space. President Kennedy announces US plans to visit the Moon.

1963
Valentina Tereshkova of the USSR becomes the first woman in space.

WHAT WAS THE COLD WAR?

After World War II, the two most powerful countries in the world were the USA and the USSR. As the most powerful countries, they had the biggest say in how the world was going to be run. However, each country had different ideas about the future – and they could not agree. The result was a rivalry that became known as the Cold War.

★ COLD WAR CHARACTERS ★

Name: **Joseph Stalin**
Lived: **1879–1953**
Job: **Leader of USSR**

Leader of the USSR from the late 1920s, Stalin was a ruthless dictator. Millions of citizens died under his rule, but Stalin also led the USSR to victory in World War II (known in the USSR as the Great Patriotic War).

COMMUNISM V. CAPITALISM

The USSR was a communist country. Its leaders did not believe that individual citizens should own homes or businesses. They thought the state should own these things, and then make sure the benefits were shared out equally among the people. The communist leaders thought that every country should be organized in this way.

The USA's leaders believed in capitalism, the system that is used in most countries today. Capitalists think people should be free to own businesses, and that they should also be free to spend their money on homes, cars and any other possessions they want.

"LET US NOT BE DECEIVED – WE ARE TODAY IN THE MIDST OF A COLD WAR."

Presidential advisor Bernard Baruch in 1947, believed to be the first time the term 'Cold War' had been used.

★ COLD WAR CHARACTERS ★

Name: **Harry S. Truman**

Lived: **1884–1972**

Job: **President of USA**

Truman became President in April 1945, after the USA's wartime leader, Franklin D. Roosevelt, died. Truman was president until 1953. In 1947, he developed the Truman Doctrine, which said that the USA had to defend the world against communism.

INTERNATIONAL RIVALRY

At the end of World War II, Soviet forces controlled most of eastern Europe. The USSR's leaders were determined to keep this control. They thought the best way to defend themselves was to be surrounded by communist countries like their own. So they made sure communist governments were formed in any territory the USSR controlled. This became known as the Eastern Bloc.

The USA and its allies were alarmed by the spread of communism in eastern Europe. In 1947, President Truman announced that the USA would fight the spread of communist influence wherever it could. The Cold War had begun.

President Truman, shown here on the right meeting Stalin, thought the USA should fight communism. He agreed to the Marshall Plan, which released funds to help with the rebuilding of post-war Europe.

COLD WAR BATTLES

By 1949, both the USA and the USSR had nuclear weapons. A direct confrontation would have resulted in both sides being destroyed, so instead of fighting face-to-face, the two superpowers backed opposite sides in other wars. These were known as proxy wars.

HELPING THE ENEMY'S ENEMY

At first, the USA and its allies sent troops to help in these proxy wars, such as those in Korea and Vietnam, but by the mid-1970s this had mostly stopped. The USSR preferred to supply weapons and other help to communist revolutionaries around the world, but it also sometimes sent troops.

In total, more than 2.7 million US personnel served in Vietnam during the conflict.

MAJOR COLD WAR CONFLICTS

The effects of the proxy wars are still being felt today. For example, the war in Korea between 1950 and 1953 saw neither side win. As a result Korea is now split into two countries. Other major Cold War conflicts included:

★ 1946–1949 GREEK CIVIL WAR

The Greek government and army were backed by the USA and Great Britain, but it still took three years to defeat the Greek communists.

★ 1948–1949 BERLIN BLOCKADE

In 1948, the East German government prevented supplies for West Berlin from crossing East Germany. The city began to run out of food and other essentials, but was saved by a massive airlift (left).

★ 1950–1953 KOREAN WAR

The South Korean government was supported by an international force led by the USA; the North Korean communists were backed by China and the USSR.

CUBA CORREOS 30

FEBRERO 3 1974

★ 1953–1959 CUBAN REVOLUTION

Communists led by Fidel Castro (left) took power from the US-backed government.

★ 1961–1975 ANGOLAN WAR OF INDEPENDENCE

★ 1964–1974 MOZAMBICAN WAR OF INDEPENDENCE

In both countries, some of the forces fighting for independence were supported by the USSR, Cuba and other communist countries.

★ 1955–1975 VIETNAM WAR

The USA first gave support to the government in South Vietnam, then began sending hundreds of thousands of troops a year to fight. The North Vietnamese communists took 19 years to win.

★ 1965–1966 US OCCUPATION OF DOMINICAN REPUBLIC

The US decided to send in troops to make sure a left-wing government did not take power.

★ 1973 CHILEAN COUP

In 1973, the left-wing government of Salvador Allende was overthrown by the military, after a long economic campaign against Chile by the USA.

THE END OF THE COLD WAR

Between 1989 and 1991, the communist governments of eastern Europe were washed from power on a wave of popular unrest.

A NEW OPENNESS

During the Cold War, whenever East Europeans tried to act independently of the USSR they were crushed. Either their own leaders or the USSR used military force to keep control. At the end of the 1980s, though, this changed. From 1985, the USSR had a new leader: Mikhail Gorbachev. Gorbachev introduced the polices of *perestroika* (restructuring) and *glasnost* (openness). Perestroika made it possible for non-communists to stand in elections for the first time. Glasnost allowed Russians to say what they really thought about things.

In other communist countries, people became angry that their leaders were not allowing them the same rights. They began to protest on the streets. This was safer than ever before, because the protesters knew that the USSR would not intervene.

★ COLD WAR CHARACTERS ★

Name: **Mikhael Gorbachev**
Lived: **1931–**
Job: **Leader of the USSR**

Gorbachev was elected General Secretary of the Communist Party in 1985. He was the first communist leader to have been born after the Russian Revolution of 1917. He introduced policies that led to the end of the Cold War and the break-up of the USSR.

THE FALL OF COMMUNISM

September 1989

The leaders of the Solidarity movement in Poland form the first post-communist government.

October

Hungary declares it is now run by a non-communist government.

November

East Germans are allowed freedom to travel.

BREAK-UP OF THE USSR

The last of Europe's communist governments to fall was the USSR itself. Glasnost meant that people were free to say what they thought. In many parts of the USSR, they thought that independence for their region would be a good idea. Right across the country people began to protest, demanding independence.

In a panic, communist military officers kidnapped President Gorbachev. They announced that he was too ill to remain in power. People did not believe this, and the protests grew still larger. After three days, the military officers gave in and Gorbachev was released. By December, he had resigned, and by January 1992 the USSR no longer existed. In its place was an alliance of countries called the Commonwealth of Independent States (CIS).

BELARUS

UKRAINE

KAZAKHSTAN

MOLDOVA

ARMENIA

GEORGIA

AZERBAIJAN

UZBEKISTAN

TURKMENISTAN

TAJIKSTAN

KYRGYZSTAN

The CIS was made up of states that had once formed the USSR, including Ukraine, Georgia, Armenia and Uzbekistan.

"THE SOCIAL AND POLITICAL ORDER IN SOME COUNTRIES CHANGED IN THE PAST, AND IT CAN CHANGE IN THE FUTURE TOO, BUT THIS IS ENTIRELY A MATTER FOR EACH PEOPLE TO DECIDE."

Mikhail Gorbachev spells out the USSR's decision not to interfere in other countries, July 1989.

December

The wall dividing West Berlin from East Germany is demolished.
The Romanian Communist Party gives up power. Czechoslovakia forms a non-Communist government. Romania's people topple the communist government of Nicolae Ceausescu.

October 1990

German reunification is approved.

COLD WAR POLITICS

★ COLD WAR CHARACTERS ★

**Andrei
Sakharov
1921-1989
Nuclear scientist**

Sakharov was the USSR's
leading nuclear scientist. He
was also a dissident –
someone who disagreed with
the government and was
prepared to say so.
As punishment, he was
banished to the city of Gorky
in 1980. When he went on a
hunger strike to protest,
Sakharov was force fed. In
1986, he was finally allowed
to go home to Moscow by
Mikhail Gorbachev.

Politics is about how countries and the world
should be run. The two sides in the Cold War
disagreed almost completely about how this
should be done. As a result, each tried to show
their own political system in a good light, while
making the other side's system look as bad as
possible. The Cold War still affects politics –
especially international politics – today.

POLITICS IN COMMUNIST COUNTRIES

Eastern Bloc leaders were convinced that only communism could
lead to a fairer way or life for everyone – so the only political
party they allowed was the Communist Party. You could elect
anyone you wanted – as long as they were a member of the
Communist Party.

Anyone thought to be disloyal to the Communist Party was likely
to be branded a traitor. In the 1930s, Stalin had said that a
criminal's family was as guilty as the criminal: if you were
arrested, your whole family would suffer. Those guilty of
speaking or writing against the Party were severely punished.
They could be sent to forced-labor camps, imprisoned or even
killed. People knew that the police had informers everywhere,
which meant a careless word could get you arrested.

QUESTION: "COMRADE, WHAT
IS THE DEFINITION OF CAPITALISM?"

ANSWER: "A SYSTEM WHERE MAN
EXPLOITS MAN."

Q: "AND WHAT IS COMMUNISM?"

A: "AH, COMMUNISM.
COMMUNISM IS THE EXACT OPPOSITE."

A Cold War joke, said to have been
popular in communist countries

★ COLD WAR CHARACTERS ★

Name: **Joseph McCarthy**
Lived: **1908–1957**
Job: **US Senator**

Senator McCarthy was a prominent campaigner against communism in the 1950s. He fought communist influence wherever he saw, or thought he saw, it. His hunt for communist influence became known as 'McCarthyism'. Today, many Americans feel that McCarthyism went too far, and that the 'crimes' it uncovered were often not really crimes at all.

POLITICS IN THE WEST

In the West, there were hundreds of political parties, and people could vote for any of them. In most countries, however, there were only two or three parties with a chance of forming the government.

Whichever party was in power, the Cold War dominated politics in a way that is hard to imagine today. Political leaders said that the fight against communism was a fight for freedom and democracy. In the USA and other allied countries, people who were thought to be communist sympathizers were harassed and persecuted.

"THESE ARE THE STAKES! TO MAKE A WORLD IN WHICH ALL OF GOD'S CHILDREN CAN LIVE, OR TO GO INTO THE DARK."

From Lyndon Baines Johnson's 1964 campaign to be elected President of the USA. People would have understood 'the dark' to mean either communism or death.

Lyndon Baines Johnson (known as 'LBJ') became president after John F. Kennedy's assassination in 1963.

INTERNATIONAL POLITICS

In Europe, the USSR and its allies built a border defense against the western capitalists. This border also stopped their citizens from moving to the West. It soon became known as the 'Iron Curtain'. The countries on each side organized themselves into two military groups, or alliances. They were the North Atlantic Treaty Organization (NATO) and the Warsaw Pact.

WESTERN ALLIANCE

NATO was formed in 1949. The first members were Belgium, Canada, Denmark, France, Iceland, Italy, Luxembourg, Netherlands, Norway, Portugal, the UK and the USA. The members changed over time. For example, West Germany joined in 1955 and France withdrew in the late 1950s. The members agreed to act together to protect one another from attack. Through NATO, the USA was able to position nuclear weapons in European countries. From western Europe, these weapons would be able to reach the USSR.

PORTUGAL

SPAIN

THE WARSAW PACT

After West Germany joined NATO in 1955, the communist countries made an alliance called the Warsaw Pact. Its members were Albania, Bulgaria, East Germany, Czechoslovakia, Hungary, Poland, Romania and the USSR.

Soviet leader Nikita Khrushchev (left) and US Vice President Richard Nixon (right) meet in 1959.

Yugoslavia did not join the Warsaw Pact. It was communist, but would not follow the USSR's leadership.

"WHETHER YOU LIKE IT OR NOT, HISTORY IS ON OUR SIDE. WE WILL BURY YOU!"

Nikita Khrushchev, leader of the USSR 1955–1964, speaking to western ambassadors in Moscow in1956.

A Divided Europe, 1985

- NATO countries and US allies
- Warsaw PACT

NORWAY

GREAT BRITAIN

EAST GERMANY

WEST GERMANY

POLAND

CZECHOSLOVAKIA

FRANCE

HUNGARY

ITALY

The 'Iron Curtain'

ROMANIA

BULGARIA

UKRAINE

GREECE

TURKEY

AFTER THE COLD WAR

Since the Cold War ended, Russia has generally opposed former communist countries joining NATO or allying themselves with western Europe. Even so, between 1999 and 2009, 12 former communist countries joined NATO. Some have also joined the European Union.

In recent years, Russia has tried to keep former communist countries under its influence. This is especially true of places that were once part of the USSR, such as Ukraine.

In 2014, protesters forced Ukraine's pro-Russian president, Yiktor Yanukovych, to flee the country. The protesters wanted Ukraine to have stronger trade links with Europe, and to escape from Russian influence. It triggered an armed conflict between pro-Europeans in western Ukraine (above) and pro-Russians in the east.

17

CONFLICTS AROUND THE WORLD

Political disagreements between capitalists and communists did not take place only in Europe. The USA and USSR battled to influence politics everywhere, from Asia to the Arctic. Many of these political conflicts became violent, with the two sides using force to try and make sure their political system took power.

Fidel Castro

★ LATIN AMERICA

In 1958–1959, communist forces led by Fidel Castro took power in Cuba. After this, the USSR used Cuba to send aid to left-wing groups in countries throughout Latin America, such as El Salvador.

At the same time, the USA supported right-wing leaders in other Latin American countries. Sometimes, these regimes were violent and oppressive, but the USA was more concerned that these right-wing leaders fought against communism.

After the Cold War, Cuba carried on as a communist country. The USA continued to campaign against Cuba, imposing restrictions on trade and travel. Elsewhere in Latin America, the political extremists became less powerful, or disappeared.

"A VICTORY OF ANY COUNTRY OVER [CAPITALISM] IS OUR VICTORY; JUST AS ANY COUNTRY'S DEFEAT IS A DEFEAT FOR ALL OF US."

Ernesto 'Che' Guevara (left), Latin American revolutionary, explains why communists around the world should support each other.

18

★ AFRICA

In Africa, the USSR and its allies supported armed groups in Ethiopia, Angola (flag pictured left) and elsewhere. As in Latin America, the USA and its allies supported right-wing governments that would fight communism. At the end of the Cold War, there was no more communist aid for the rebel groups. It became harder for them to continue fighting, but not all died out.

★ THE MIDDLE EAST

The Middle East is an important source of oil, which made it another important Cold War battleground. Both sides supplied weapons or other support to friendly governments. When this stopped, the governments in countries such as Syria, Iraq and Afghanistan were weakened. The effect has been to create instability in the region.

★ ASIA

Asia was a major Cold War battleground. This was where the most famous proxy wars were fought, in Korea (1950–1953) and Vietnam (1955–1975) – this image shows US troops during the Vietnam War. Communists won power in North Korea and Vietnam, and communist governments are still in charge there. India had strong links to the USSR during the Cold War, and today still has a close relationship with Russia.

"HEY! HEY! LBJ! HOW MANY KIDS DID YOU KILL TODAY?"

Protesters against the Vietnam War chanting at President Lyndon Baines Johnson in 1968.

AFTER THE COLD WAR

Armed conflicts have largely died out in Latin America and Asia. In the Middle East and Central Africa, though, the end of the Cold War left a power vacuum. As a result, small-scale conflicts have sprung up and claimed millions of lives.

During the 1960s and 1970s, many protests were held in western countries against the US's role in the Vietnam War.

LIFE IN THE EAST

Today, it is hard to imagine the effect the Cold War had on people's lives. In the Eastern Bloc, life was hard for most citizens. They lacked many of the freedoms and comforts we take for granted. In the West, the fear of nuclear attack was ever-present. Some of the effects of the Cold War are still being felt by ordinary people around the world today.

LIFE IN THE EASTERN BLOC

In the Eastern Bloc, everyone's life was rigidly controlled. There were few goods in the shops, and almost no one had a car. TV, newspapers, movies and books were all controlled by the Communist Party. All businesses and industries were owned by the state, so the government decided who worked where, and how much they earned. People's homes were also owned by the state, and most people lived in poor-quality apartments.

The exceptions to this were Party officials and leading citizens, such as sports stars and great scientists. They often lived in the best apartments, and had access to cars and other goods.

The Trabant was built in East Germany as an affordable car for ordinary people. More than 3 million were made.

DEFECTING TO THE WEST

Leaving the Eastern Bloc and moving to a capitalist country was called 'defecting'. Defecting was a crime, and the punishment was severe: you could be imprisoned for years, or even killed. But fear of punishment was not enough to stop people defecting, so the authorities built impassable barriers all along their borders with the West.

The most famous barrier was the Berlin Wall (left), which surrounded West Berlin between 1961 and 1989. Before 1961, about 3.5 million East Germans had left for a new life in the West. Many did this by crossing into West Berlin. After the Berlin Wall was built, few people managed to defect – though hundreds of people were killed while trying.

> "LEAVING [EAST GERMANY] IS AN ACT OF POLITICAL AND MORAL BACKWARDNESS AND DEPRAVITY."
> East German government propaganda leaflet, 1955.

Building of the Berlin Wall started in August 1961. In East Germany, it was officially known as the 'Anti-Fascist Protection Rampart'.

★ COLD WAR CHARACTERS ★

Name: **Roman Abramovich**

Lived: **1966–**

Job: **Oligarch**

Roman Abramovich is just one of the Russian oligarchs who became rich after the Cold War ended. He did this by buying oil and gas businesses that had been owned by the state. They cost millions of dollars – but their value soon increased to billions, making Abramovich one of the world's wealthiest men.

AFTER THE COLD WAR

After the Cold War, people in the old Eastern Bloc got the freedoms most had been hoping for. They also got a new set of problems. Without government support, everything from roads and airports to the health service and schools began to run out of cash. At the same time, many government assets were sold to individuals who became fabulously rich. These people became known as oligarchs.

LIFE IN THE WEST

In the West, life was very different from the Eastern Bloc. For most people, things were very similar to today. They had the freedom to travel, they could own their own homes and they had access to all kinds of products, as long as they could afford them. They could say and write almost whatever they liked – but supporting communism could still land you in trouble.

THE NUCLEAR MENACE

One fear that hung over the West was the threat of nuclear attack. Since 1949, the USSR had had nuclear weapons. As space technology developed, both sides in the Cold War began to make powerful rockets, which could be used to carry nuclear warheads huge distances. By the 1970s, both the USA and USSR had developed missiles that could travel more than 3,400 miles (5,500 km).

In the West, the nuclear build-up spread fear of a possible attack, and from the 1950s to the 1980s the dread of nuclear armageddon clouded many people's lives. In countries where the USA had based nuclear weapons, such as the UK, many people feared that this could make them a target for an attack by the Eastern Bloc.

"IT WAS A PERFECTLY BEAUTIFUL NIGHT... I WALKED OUT OF THE PRESIDENT'S OVAL OFFICE, AND AS I WALKED OUT, I THOUGHT I MIGHT NEVER SEE ANOTHER SATURDAY NIGHT."

US Secretary of Defense Robert Macnamara, wondering if the world was about to end during the Cuban Missile Crisis.

People living in the West were able to buy all sorts of luxuries, including kitchen goods and large cars.

★ EYES IN THE SKY ★

Both sides in the Cold War spent huge amounts of money creating sophisticated methods of spying on each other. One of these was the U-2 aircraft (left). Fitted with powerful spying equipment, the aircraft could fly high over the USSR recording information about the territory beneath.

However, during one such flight in May 1960, Soviet missiles succeeded in bringing down one of the aircraft. The pilot, Gary Powers, was captured and tried for spying. In 1962, he was exchanged for a Soviet spy who was being held prisoner by the USA.

THE CUBAN MISSILE CRISIS

For 13 days in October 1962, many people feared that the world was on the brink of nuclear war. The cause was nuclear missiles the USSR wanted to base in Cuba. These would have been able to attack the USA, which demanded the missiles be removed. After a tense stand-off, the USSR backed down and in return, the USA promised that it would never try to invade Cuba.

Nikita Khrushchev (right) and Cuban leader Fidel Castro.

Range of long-range missiles 1,988miles (3,200 km)

CANADA

New York

Washington DC

Key

🔋 Cuban missile site

– – US naval blockade of Cuba

➡ Approaching Soviet ships

Range of short-range missiles 994 miles (1,600 km)

USA

MEXICO

CUBA

23

CUBA AND VIETNAM

During the Cold War, the Eastern Bloc supported countries that were communist, sympathetic to communism, or just anti-American. It helped them by supplying weapons, but also by trying to make life better for their people. This was a way of showing that communism was a better system than capitalism.

When the Cold War ended and the USSR collapsed, this help disappeared. In some places, such as Cuba, the effect was disastrous. Other places, such as Vietnam, adjusted more easily to the new post-Cold War world.

CUBA AFTER THE COLD WAR

Cuba's communist government had been supported by the USSR since taking power in 1959. Cuba needed foreign currency to pay for goods from abroad, such as medicines and farming machinery. To help with this problem, the USSR sold oil to Cuba at reduced prices. Cuba could then either use the oil, or re-sell it at higher prices to make money. The USSR also bought sugar and other goods from Cuba at guaranteed high prices.

When the USSR's communist government fell, the money flowing to Cuba stopped. New buyers for Cuba's goods were hard to find. This was because the USA – now the world's most powerful country – said that anyone who wanted to trade with the USA could not also trade with Cuba.

Ordinary Cubans began to go hungry. There was no electricity for days on end, and no gas for cars or buses.

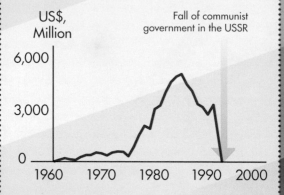

CUBAN AID BEFORE 1989

Economic assistance from the Soviet Union to Cuba 1960–2000.

US$, Million

Fall of communist government in the USSR

6,000

3,000

0

1960   1970   1980   1990   2000

Since the end of the Vietnam War, Ho Chi Minh City has developed into a modern capital city.

Many people in Cuba drive antique American cars, which they have to maintain by making their own spare parts.

VIETNAM AFTER THE COLD WAR

Like Cuba, Vietnam had also been supported by the Eastern Bloc. When the USSR collapsed, it caused Vietnam serious problems. However, Vietnam has dealt with the change more successfully than Cuba. One of the reasons is that the USA's attitude to Vietnam is more friendly than its attitude to Cuba.

Links between the two countries have grown since the end of the Vietnam War, and today the USA is Vietnam's main trading partner. As a result, some Vietnamese living in cities have become wealthy. They own property, and buy modern luxury goods, electronics and other gadgets. In the countryside, people are still mostly poor. The communist government is still in power, and clamps down harshly on any opposition.

In 2000, President Bill Clinton became the first US president to visit Vietnam since America's defeat in the war of 1955–1975.

THE ARMS RACE

As tensions between the USA and the Soviet Union grew during the Cold War, each began building up their military strength. Whether it was weapons, planes, aircraft carriers or soldiers, neither side could afford to let the other get too far ahead. The two superpowers were in a constant race to overtake each other militarily. Both stockpiled enough nuclear weapons to destroy the world several times over.

NUCLEAR WEAPONS

The USA first used nuclear bombs in 1945. At Hiroshima and Nagasaki in Japan, single bombs flattened huge areas of each city, killing over 100,000 people. Nuclear warheads are the most powerful weapons ever developed – and they became the most important weapon of the Cold War.

The USSR set off its first atomic bomb in 1949. From then on, each side in the Cold War built up increasingly large stockpiles of nuclear weapons. These could be fired in rockets, dropped from aircraft, or even launched from submarines.

> "A WORLD WITHOUT NUCLEAR WEAPONS WOULD BE LESS STABLE AND MORE DANGEROUS FOR ALL OF US."
>
> Margaret Thatcher, British Prime Minister 1979–1990.

This is a replica of the nuclear bomb dropped on the Japanese city of Nagasaki on August 9, 1945. The device was nicknamed 'Fat Man'.

A MAD WORLD

The build-up of weapons was based on a policy that in the USA was called MAD. This was short for 'Mutually Assured Destruction'. The idea was that with such deadly arsenals on each side, it would be impossible for anyone to win a nuclear war. Instead, both sides – and possibly the whole world – would be destroyed. This terrible possibility would ensure that nuclear war did not actually happen.

Russia and the USA still keep powerful rockets ready to launch at a moment's notice and carry nuclear weapons to the other side of the world. These rockets are called Intercontinental Ballistic Missiles (ICBMs).

LIMITING NUCLEAR WEAPONS

The build-up of nuclear weapons eventually became so great that even the two enemies realized it should not carry on. In 1970, the Treaty on the Non-Proliferation of Nuclear Weapons came into force. Signed by the UK, USA and USSR, the treaty aimed to stop the spread of nuclear weapons technology and reduce the number of weapons. Even so, the number of warheads increased as more countries developed their own nuclear weapons.

NON-NUCLEAR FORCES

As well as nuclear weapons, each side built up its 'conventional' forces. These included soldiers, tanks, guns, aircraft, battleships and submarines. The USSR's army (above) was estimated to have between 4 and 5 million soldiers during most of the Cold War. The US Army usually had fewer than a million soldiers, but they tended to be better trained and equipped with more advanced weapons.

> "A WORLD FREE OF NUCLEAR WEAPONS WILL BE SAFER AND MORE PROSPEROUS."
>
> Ban Ki-moon,
> UN Secretary
> General since 2007.

NUCLEAR ARMS RACE

The world's nuclear arsenals ballooned throughout the Cold War:

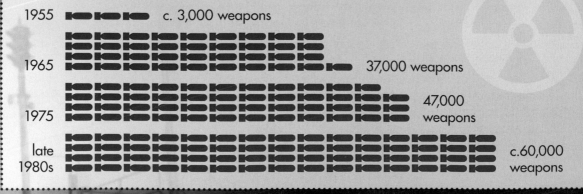

1955 — c. 3,000 weapons

1965 — 37,000 weapons

1975 — 47,000 weapons

late 1980s — c.60,000 weapons

NUCLEAR LEGACY OF THE COLD WAR

As a result of the Cold War, there are a lot of nuclear weapons in the world. Almost all are held by either the USA or Russia, but at least seven other countries have also developed them. Among them is North Korea, which despite pressure from other countries has continued working on nuclear weapons carried by missiles. Iran, too, is said to want to develop nuclear warheads.

NUCLEAR POWER

Some of the technology developed during the nuclear arms race is today used in a peaceful way, to provide electricity. By 2012, more than 12 percent of the world's electricity was being produced by nuclear power stations.

WORLD NUCLEAR WEAPONS, 2015

South Africa is the only country that has given up its nuclear weapons, when it decommissioned them in 1991. Israel has never formally admitted to having nuclear weapons.

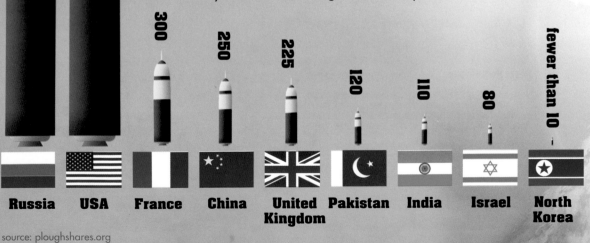

Russia	USA	France	China	United Kingdom	Pakistan	India	Israel	North Korea
7,500	7,100	300	250	225	120	110	80	fewer than 10

source: ploughshares.org

NUCLEAR TESTING

During the Cold War, several countries carried out nuclear tests as a way of developing bombs. Between 1955 and 1989, an average of 55 nuclear tests were carried out every year.

A satellite image of Bikini Atoll in the Pacific Ocean. It was used by the USA as a test site for nuclear devices.

Crater formed by nuclear test explosion

These tests usually took place in remote locations, such as deserts or isolated islands. One problem with nuclear testing was that the bombs released dangerous radioactive fallout, which stayed around for a long time. For example, the USA's largest-ever nuclear bomb was set off in the Marshall Islands, a remote part of the Pacific Ocean, in 1954. Three inhabited islands were poisoned by radioactive fallout, and had to be abandoned. They are still thought to be contaminated today.

As a result of the dangers of nuclear testing, in 1963 the Partial Test Ban Treaty was agreed to and signed. This stops any nuclear testing underwater, in space and in the atmosphere. Only underground tests are allowed. The treaty is still in place today.

EXPERIMENTS ON CITIZENS

As well as nuclear tests, governments on both sides of the Cold War tested other kinds of weapons. Sometimes they even did tests on their own citizens without warning them. The tests included experimenting on soldiers to see what effect chemical weapons would have, and spraying the city of San Francisco with bacteria (shown here magnified thousands of times) to simulate an attack by biological weapons.

29

THE SPACE RACE

The Space Race was an important part of the Cold War technology battle. In the 1950s, the USA and the USSR both wanted to send the first satellite into orbit. Unaware of the progress the Soviets were making in their research, the USA got a terrible shock in 1961, when the USSR's Yuri Gagarin became the first human in space. The USA was spurred into action. It decided to invest billions of dollars into landing a human on the Moon (see pages 4–5), which it achieved in 1969.

A propaganda poster from the USSR celebrating their achievements in space exploration.

LEGACIES OF THE SPACE RACE

Of course, rockets that could carry a human into space had another use. They could also carry nuclear weapons over huge distances. But not all the products of the space race were warlike – quite a few are everyday things that might surprise you:

★ BARCODES

In the old days, the price of every product in a store had to be keyed in by hand. With the rise of supermarkets, people began looking into making this process automatic. NASA had been using something called 'barcodes', such as this one, as a way of keeping track of the thousands of parts that went into a spacecraft. This same system was adapted for recording how much supermarket goods cost.

1969
Neil Armstrong and Buzz Aldrin become the first humans to walk on the Moon.

1971
The USSR launches Saylut 1, the first-ever space station.

★ SATELLITE TV

At first, NASA Mission Control communicated with astronauts using a network of high-level weather balloons. This proved unreliable, so scientists developed satellite communications technology (left) as a better way of keeping in touch. That same technology is the basis for the satellite TV many people have in their homes today.

★ THE JOYSTICK

Astronauts used a Lunar Rover to get around on the Moon. Having to use two hands for steering would have been unsafe – an astronaut needed one hand free at all times. So scientists developed the joystick as a way of controlling the Rover, which later evolved into joysticks for playing computer games (left).

★ ATHLETIC SHOES

Technology from the first Moon boots made its way into many sports shoes, such as the one shown here. In particular, shock-absorbing, stability control midsoles found in running shoes are based on shoe technology developed during the Space Race.

COLD WAR CHARACTERS ★

Name: **Yuri Gagarin**
Lived: **1934-1968**
Job: **Cosmonaut**

Gagarin was the first person ever to visit outer space, in 1961. He was made a Hero of the Soviet Union, the USSR's highest honor, and became an international celebrity. Gagarin became Director of the Cosmonaut Training Center, but died in a jet-fighter crash at the age of just 34.

The powerful Saturn V rocket was developed to carry the Apollo Moon missions. Its chief designer, Wernher von Braun, had designed rockets for Nazi Germany during World War II. After the war, von Braun and other German rocket scientists were brought to the USA to continue their work.

The Space Shuttle was in service from 1981 until its retirement in 2011.

1971
A Soviet probe, Mars 2, becomes the first human-made object on Mars.

1973
The US spacecraft Pioneer 10 performs the first flyby of Jupiter.

1981
The USA launches the first Space Shuttle.

THE SPY GAME

In 1946, a group of Moscow schoolchildren visited the US Ambassador to the USSR. As a present, they brought him a wooden model of the Great Seal of the United States. The Ambassador was so pleased that he hung the Great Seal in his office. But in 1952, a bug was discovered hidden inside the Seal. Spies from the USSR had been listening to secret ambassadorial conversations for the last six years. In the Cold War, each side was desperate to know what the other was up to. To find out, they trained secret armies of spies, and developed some amazing technology for these spies to use.

The large wooden seal hung above the desk of the US Ambassador in Moscow.

★ LISTENING DEVICES

The Great Seal was an ingenious idea, but at 2 feet (0.6 m) across it was hard to hide. Both sides developed tiny listening devices for secretly listening to conversations. These could be planted in light fittings, telephones and electrical sockets. There was even a watch containing a secret microphone.

Microphones hidden in the mouthpiece and earpiece of a telephone could record everything that was said and heard.

★ SPY WEAPONS

As well as ordinary guns, spies had a whole arsenal of special weapons they could use in a tight spot. A glove-gun, hidden under a long sleeve, could be used to fire a single shot. Female agents from the Eastern Bloc carried lipstick guns: turning the bottom of the lipstick fired a bullet out of the top. There was an umbrella that fired poison darts from its tip (left)and there was even a tiny weapons kit that was designed to be hidden up a spy's bottom.

★ MEDICAL TECHNOLOGY ★

Medical technology developed significantly during the Cold War. Nuclear research led to breakthroughs in our understanding and treatment of cancer. Cold War science also helped develop medical imaging technology, such as MRI scanners (above). These let doctors see what is happening inside someone's body without cutting them open. And one side-effect of the wars in Korea and Vietnam was that doctors learned a lot about how to treat battlefield injuries.

★ ALL KINDS OF CAMERAS

Hidden cameras were a great way of secretly recording information. All kinds of tiny cameras were developed. There were cameras in the handles of walking sticks, ones that could be placed in the heel of a shoe, or tucked behind a tie, or even hidden in a bird box.

The heel of this shoe has been swivelled back to reveal a tiny hidden camera.

33

SCIENCE AND TECHNOLOGY

The US government poured a lot of money into its military during the Cold War to make sure it was as technologically advanced as the Soviets'. This led to a number of innovations that proved hugely beneficial to the wider population. For instance, the Internet began as a computer network for military research, while GPS satellite navigation had its origins in the USA's attempts to track the first Soviet satellite, Sputnik.

BIRTH OF THE INTERNET

In order to compete technologically with the Soviets, the USA realized that its research institutions had to be able to share knowledge easily. So in 1969, ARPA (Advanced Projects Research Agency), a branch of the military, set up ARPANET, a computer network linking several research laboratories across the country (the image shows Leonard Kleinrock, one of the computer scientists behind ARPANET). Over the next few years, more and more institutions, hooked up to the network. The computer technology became the basis for the Internet.

★ EMAIL

ARPA (see below left) was behind several Cold War computing breakthroughs. In 1971, the ARPA programr Ray Tomlinson devised a way of sending electronic mail – or email – between computers. The first email was sent between two computers sitting next to each other. Tomlinson also came up with the idea of using the '@' sign in email addresses.

★ COMPUTER MOUSE

Finding your way around a computer screen became a lot easier in 1963 when Douglas Engelbart, an engineer at the Augmentation Research Center (a body funded by ARPA), created the first computer mouse (left) using a block of wood and two small wheels.

★ CRASH TEST DUMMIES

The crash test dummy (left) was first developed in 1949 for the US Air Force. However, the idea soon attracted the attention of the nation's car manufacturers who began making their own, modified for automobiles, in the 1960s.

A network of satellites in orbit around Earth can pinpoint your position to within a few yards.

★ GLOBAL POSITIONING SYSTEM

When Sputnik was launched in 1957, US scientists tracked its progress by measuring the frequency of its electronic signals. By doing this, they realized that it was also possible to pinpoint the locations of receivers on the ground by measuring their distance from a satellite. This realization eventually led to the development of the GPS satellite navigation system by the US military in 1972. The public were given access to the technology in the 1980s. Today, GPS receivers in phones (below) and SatNav devices pinpoint your position by measuring the rate of radio signals sent by four or more satellites.

PROPAGANDA

Both sides in the Cold War set up institutions to promote the superiority of their political system using propaganda. Culture played an important role in this process. In the Soviet Union, writers and musicians were ordered by the State to make art praising the Communist system. In the West, the pressure was less direct, but artists were still heavily influenced by the Cold War, creating stories and characters that reflected current events.

COMINFORM AND THE 'PEACE OFFENSIVE'

This is the logo for Cominform, an organization set up in 1947 to help link together Eastern Bloc governments, It also tried to encourage other countries to become communists. During the early 1950s, Cominform started a 'peace offensive'. It secretly supported groups in the West that campaigned for peace and disarmament. It also secretly helped cultural organizations that were sympathetic to communism, or were a thorn in their government's side.

A statue of cosmonaut Yuri Gagarin, created in a style typical of the USSR.

THE CONGRESS FOR CULTURAL FREEDOM

Members of the Congress meet to celebrate its tenth anniversary in June 1960.

In 1950, partly in response to Cominform's activities, the USA created the Congress for Cultural Freedom. The Congress had offices in 35 countries, employed dozens of people, supported more than 20 magazines, art exhibitions, a news service, international conferences, and musicians and artists. It did all this with the aim of spreading the American way of life.

A Soviet poster from the 1960s showing support for North Vietnam. It says 'We're in solidarity with you, Vietnam.'

МЫ СОЛИДАРНЫ С ТОБОЙ, ВЬЕТНАМ!

★ COLD WAR CHARACTERS ★

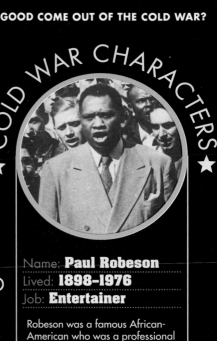

Name: **Paul Robeson**

Lived: **1898–1976**

Job: **Entertainer**

Robeson was a famous African-American who was a professional athlete, a law graduate, an actor and singer. He was also an early civil rights campaigner. Robeson was sympathetic to left-wing causes – so during the 1950s the government confiscated his passport and he was blacklisted.

"THE KGB HELPED TO FUND JUST ABOUT EVERY ANTIWAR MOVEMENT AND ORGANIZATION IN AMERICA AND ABROAD."

Former Soviet official Stanislav Lunev, writing in 1998.

The pop artist Andy Warhol (above) created art out of everyday objects, such as Campbell's soup cans.

ART AND THE COLD WAR

In the USA, a new kind of art called abstract expressionism developed after World War II. Its paintings were unlike anything seen before – many people doubted if they were even art. Some abstract expressionists were sympathetic to the Eastern Bloc – which makes it surprising that they were supported (in secret) by the US government. The reason was that the USA wanted to show itself as a place where creative ideas were encouraged. This was a contrast to the USSR, where artists' work was strictly controlled by the government. Later, in the 1950s and 1960s, a form of art called Pop Art developed. It reflected many of the changes and concerns of the Cold War. New products such as TVs and washing machines, colorful advertising, celebrities such as Marilyn Monroe, space and war were all themes in the Pop artists' work.

POPULAR CULTURE

In the Cold War, the two sides knew that people were deeply affected by the music they listened to, the TV shows and movies they watched, the art they saw, and even the sports teams they supported. Impressing people in these areas of life was a good way of encouraging them to support your side.

★ SCIENCE FICTION BOOKS AND COMICS

Science fiction writers try to imagine what the future will be like. Since the Cold War was a battle for the future world, sci-fi became an important form of writing. In the Eastern Bloc, writers were expected to show a perfect future, in which communism had triumphed. In the West, science fiction novels and comics often showed a future where technology gave humans a life of ease and luxury. It also featured heroes who had developed amazing new powers.

> "JUST NOW I WAS TOLD THAT I COULD NOT GO TO DISNEYLAND. I ASKED 'WHY NOT? WHAT IS IT, DO YOU HAVE ROCKET LAUNCHING PADS THERE?'"
>
> Nikita Khrushchev misses out on the fun while visiting the USA.

★ POP MUSIC

In June 1987, David Bowie (left) was the headline act of a three-day pop festival staged in West Berlin right next to the Berlin Wall. A huge crowd of dancing East Germans gathered on the other side chanting, 'The Wall must fall! The Wall must fall!'. Two-and-a-half years later, the Wall had been pulled down. It did not happen because of the concert, but the events of June 1987 did show how important music was to both sides. For many young people in the Eastern Bloc, Western pop music was a symbol of a free world they wanted to join. To their leaders, pop music represented everything that was bad about the 'decadent' West.

★ CINEMA AND TV

By the 1960s, cinema and TV were used by both sides in the Cold War to encourage support from their own citizens, or to show the other side in a bad light.

In the Eastern Bloc, cinema was tightly controlled by the government. In the USSR, the West was usually shown as villainous. In fact, between 1946 and 1950, nearly half of the baddies in Soviet films were either American or British.

★ COLD WAR CHARACTERS

Name: **Iron Man, Hulk, Fantastic Four, Captain America, X-Men**

Lived: **Various**

Job: **Comic-book characters**

Many comic-book heroes first appeared during the Cold War, though today their backstories have sometimes been changed. For example: Hulk was created during a weapons test; Iron Man first developed his armor in Vietnam (later changed to Afghanistan); and the Fantastic Four originally got their powers as part of the Space Race.

★ SPY STORIES

Spies were a popular subject for Cold War writers. In the West, the most famous fictional spy is James Bond (left), but many others were also popular. In Russia, the equivalent of Bond is a spy called Maksim Isaev. His adventures were made into a TV series. This is said to be so popular in Russia that when it is shown, the crime rate drops because everyone is indoors watching TV.

SPORTS RIVALRY

Both sides in the Cold War knew that sporting success could have a big effect on their people. If your country's hockey team did well, it made everyone feel happier. If one of your boxers became world champion, people felt just a bit tougher. And if the loser was from the other side in the Cold War, that was even better. As a result, countries on both sides made great efforts to achieve sporting glory. From the chessboard to the swimming pool, the football pitch to the gymnastics mat, East battled West for sporting success.

DRUG ABUSE IN SPORT

In the Eastern Bloc, young people were selected to attend special sports schools, often hundreds or even thousands of miles from home. There they trained every day, with the finest coaches and the best technology their country could provide. We now know that part of their training sometimes included the use of outlawed drugs, such as anabolic steroids.

"BEFORE COMPETITIONS, WE GOT INJECTIONS EVERY DAY. WITHIN 2–3 HOURS, YOU COULD FEEL YOUR BODY GETTING WARMER. BUT THE COACHES DIDN'T TELL US WHAT IT WAS."

Former East German cyclist Uwe Trömer describes being given illegal drugs by his coaches.

The drugs were often given to the athletes without their knowledge. One report says that 90 percent of East Germany's doped athletes now have health problems as a result. In East Germany, the doping program even had an official name: State Plan 14.25. Athletes from the West also used illegal drugs, but there is no evidence that it was planned in the same way as in the Eastern Bloc.

East German shot putter Heidi Kreiger was given anabolic steroids by her coaches and began to develop male characteristics. Heidi later had a sex-change operation and became Andreas Kreiger.

COLD WAR CONTESTS

★ 1956
'BLOOD IN THE WATER' WATER POLO

Weeks before this 1956 Olympic water polo match between Hungary and the USSR, the USSR had invaded its 'ally' to put down protests. Each team had a point to make – but the Hungarians made theirs more strongly. After one of the most violent games ever played, they finished 4–0 winners.

★ 1972
CHESS MASTERS

In 1972, Soviet defending chess champion Boris Spassky was challenged by the USA's Bobby Fischer (right). Despite never having beaten Spassky before, Fischer won by 12.5 points to 8.5, and became the world's first superstar chess player.

★ 1976
COMANECI'S 10

Romania's Nadja Comaneci (left) was just 14 when she entered the gymnastics arena at the 1976 Olympics. Few people outside the world of gymnastics had heard of her. That changed when she scored the first ever 10 – the highest score possible – on the uneven bars. Comaneci went on to score 10 another six times and become the most popular Eastern Bloc athlete the world has seen.

Comaneci won a total of five Olympic gold medals – three at Montreal and two more at the 1980 games in Moscow.

★ 1980 AND 1984
OLYMPIC BOYCOTTS

The 1980 Olympic Games was held in Moscow, capital of the USSR. The previous year, Soviet forces had invaded Afghanistan; as a protest, the USA and several other western countries did not send athletes to the Olympics. In retaliation, the USSR and its allies refused to attend the 1984 Olympics in Los Angeles.

AFTER THE COLD WAR

The Cold War, like any conflict, was a bad thing. In the Eastern Bloc, millions of people were denied a choice about who governed them. Citizens were punished severely if they disagreed with their government. The Cold War fuelled armed conflicts around the world, from Latin America to Africa and Asia. So, the end of the Cold War was a good thing – but it did have some bad outcomes.

> "WE ARE FINDING OUT THAT WHAT LOOKED LIKE A NEGLECTED HOUSE A YEAR AGO IS IN FACT A RUIN."

Vaclav Havel, first President of the Czech Republic, speaking in 1991 about conditions in former Eastern Bloc countries after the fall of communism.

ECONOMIC PROBLEMS

The economies of the old Eastern Bloc countries were not ready for the end of communism. Their industries, agriculture and other businesses were not used to being part of a capitalist economy, where they had to compete against others. They were like an athlete who has been training alone, but is suddenly put into an Olympic training group. Many struggled to keep up.

As a result, life was hard for many citizens of former communist countries during the 1990s. Some people began to feel that life under communism had actually been better; in a few countries, the Communist Party began to make a comeback.

Writer and dissident, Vaclav Havel, became the first president of Czechoslovakia in 1989, following the fall of the communist regime there. In 1993, he became president of the Czech Republic, when the country was divided into the Czech Republic and Slovakia.

★ ILLEGAL WEAPONS SALES ★

When the Cold War ended, many countries had huge stockpiles of weapons. In wealthy places such as the USA and many western European countries, these weapons were either decommissioned or kept secure. But in former communist countries this was not always the case. Weapons were sold illegally as a way of raising money. Some of them are now being used by criminals or terrorists.

INSTABILITY AND CONFLICT

The end of the Cold War meant that both sides stopped supporting their allies around the world. In some places, this had a negative effect. Strong leaders were weakened, which gave their rivals a chance to challenge them. In the Middle East, Islamic extremists such as Al Qaeda and Islamic State have flourished, as strong regimes in Iraq, Syria and other countries have crumbled.

The break-up of the USSR has led to instability and conflict in countries that were once part of the USSR, such as Ukraine and Georgia/South Ossetia. The conflicts are over how much control Russia should have.

In 2014, anti-government protesters (right) occupied Independence Square in the heart of Ukraine's capital, Kiev. They forced the country's pro-Russian president to flee, but this led to a violent civil war in the east of the country between the new government and people who are loyal to Russia.

POSITIVE EFFECTS OF THE COLD WAR

Although wars are a bad thing, good things can come out of them. Governments are more willing to encourage new technologies than they might be in peacetime. And the products of wartime often turn out to be useful in peacetime too.

A crowd gathers around the demolished statue of Josef Stalin during the revolt in Hungary in 1956.

★TECHNOLOGY

Technological development during the Cold War was focused on weapons, but many of the developments that happened also had peacetime uses. Imagine life without computers, comfortable athletic shoes (left), treatment for cancer, satellite TV, medical scanners, or joysticks for your games controller. All these, and many more everyday products, were developed as a result of the Cold War.

★POLITICS AND INTERNATIONAL RELATIONS

Some Cold War organizations, such as NATO, still exist. Today, NATO has been joined by some former Eastern Bloc countries. NATO's recent roles have included peacekeeping missions and campaigns to limit the spread of weapons of mass destruction. Also set up during the Cold War was the Treaty on the Non-Proliferation of Nuclear Weapons, or 'Non-Proliferation Treaty'. Today this has been signed by 190 countries. They work together to stop the spread of nuclear weapons, and encourage countries that do have nuclear weapons to disarm.

NATO flag

NEW COUNTRIES AFTER 1989

These are some of the new countries that appeared after the breakup of the Eastern Bloc in 1989:

Czechoslovakia became:
Czech Republic and Slovakia.

Yugoslavia became:
Bosnia, Croatia, Macedonia, Montenegro, Serbia and Slovenia.

USSR became:
Armenia, Azerbaijan, Belarus, Estonia, Georgia, Kazakhstan, Kyrgyzstan, Latvia, Lithuania, Moldova, Russia, Tajikistan, Turkmenistan, Ukraine and Uzbekistan.

★ NEW DEMOCRACIES AND NATIONS

Under communism, Eastern Bloc countries were controlled by the USSR. They could not act independently; when Hungary tried, in 1956, the USSR invaded. After 1989, Eastern Bloc countries became democracies. They had a choice of political parties, and people could elect whatever government they wanted. When the USSR itself broke apart in 1991–1992, 15 new countries were formed (see above).

★ CULTURE

The Cold War still inspires artists and writers today. Since 2000, for example, there have been film versions of the classic Cold War spy novel *Tinker, Tailor, Soldier, Spy*, and three big TV series set in the Cold War (*The Americans*, *Allegiance* and *The Game*). The James Bond film series, inspired by books set in the Cold War, such as the one on the right, is still running. Cold War-era art by artists such as Andy Warhol remains popular.

Author Ian Fleming wrote 12 James Bond novels and two short stories.

45

GLOSSARY

armageddon
A sudden event so catastrophic that it is likely to bring about the end of the human race, or even the end of the world.

arsenal
A collection of weapons; a nuclear arsenal, for example, is the total number of nuclear weapons a country has.

asset
Something that is useful. An asset can be an item, a person or even a position.

astronaut
The Western name for someone who journeys into space.

blacklist
A list of people who are thought to be untrustworthy or unacceptable in some way. The most common use of a blacklist is to stop people getting jobs.

bug
A device for secretly listening to, and usually also recording, what people are saying.

civil rights
The rights of citizens to have the same treatment and opportunities as everyone else. Civil rights include the right to education and the right to vote.

cosmonaut
The Russian name for someone who journeys into space.

decommission
To stop something from working, and usually then to dismantle it.

defect
To leave your own country to join an enemy country.

democracy
A system where the government is chosen by a vote of nearly all the people in a country (even in democracies there are some people who cannot vote, such as children).

European Union (E.U.)
An alliance of several European countries, which have no barriers to trade or movement of people between them. Several former Eastern Bloc countries have now joined the E.U., which has made it easier for them to trade and become more wealthy.

Great Seal
A stamp used to mark official documents to show that they are real.

hunger strike
Refusing to eat; it is used as a protest or bargaining tactic.

left-wing
A broad term used to describe everything from communists to people who think the rich should pay more taxes than the poor, or that the state should provide services to those who cannot afford them.

proxy war
A war begun or supported by a powerful country, which does not take part in the war itself. The USA and USSR took opposite sides in many proxy wars during the Cold War.

reunification
Joining together of something that had been broken apart. After World War II, Germany was split into two countries, East and West Germany; it was reunified in 1990.

right-wing
A broad term used to describe those who think that the state should not interfere with people's lives, or tax richer people to help those who are poorer.

Soviet
To do with the former USSR, where a 'Soviet' was an elected council.

stockpile
A large collection or build-up of something. In the Cold War, both the USA and the USSR built up stockpiles of weapons.

USSR
Union of Soviet Socialist Republics, a country formed in 1922, after the Communist Party had taken power in Russia in 1917.

FOR MORE INFORMATION

★ BOOKS TO READ

Top Secret Files: The Cold War
Stephanie Bearce
(Prufrock Press, 2015)
Part of a series of books that reveal interesting secrets about famous historical events. This discusses secret missions and hidden facts about the main Cold War spy agencies: the KGB, CIA and MI6.

Inside the Secret World of Espionage: The Ultimate Spy
H. Keith Melton
(Dorling Kindersley, 2015)
From spy technology and the tactics of secret agents to methods of assassination, this book tells the story of spies through the ages. It is not just about the Cold War, but there is plenty of Cold War material inside.

The Cold War series
various authors (Wayland, 2002)
This series has books about major Cold War events including Causes Of The Cold War, The Vietnam War, The Cuban Missile Crisis, and more.

Secret History: The Cold War
Reg Grant
(Franklin Watts, 2010)
This book focuses on the story of spies and spying during the Cold War.

101 Facts: The Cold War
IP Factly
(IP Factly, 2014)
This book explains facts about the Cold War that might take you by surprise.

★ MUSEUMS TO VISIT

International Spy Museum
800 F St. NW, Washington DC 20004
The International Spy Museum features the largest collection of international espionage artifacts ever placed on public display. The International Spy Museum explores the craft, practice, history, and contemporary role of espionage.

Imperial War Museum
Lambeth Road
London SE1 6HZ
The Imperial War Museum features conflicts through history, including the Cold War.

WEBSITES

Because of the changing nature of Internet links, Rosen Publishing has developed an online list of websites related to the subject of this book. This site is updated regularly. Please use this link to access this list:

http://www.rosenlinks.com/INNO/Cold

INDEX